It's Easter!

by Richard Sebra

BUMBA BOOKS™

LERNER PUBLICATIONS ◆ MINNEAPOLIS

Note to Educators:

Throughout this book, you'll find critical thinking questions. These can be used to engage young readers in thinking critically about the topic and in using the text and photos to do so.

Lerner Publications Company
A division of Lerner Publishing Group, Inc.
241 First Avenue North
Minneapolis, MN 55401 USA

For reading levels and more information, look up this title at www.lernerbooks.com.

Library of Congress Cataloging-in-Publication Data

Names: Sebra, Richard, 1984- author.
Title: It's Easter! / by Richard Sebra.
Description: Minneapolis : Lerner Publications, [2017] | Series: Bumba Books — It's a Holiday! | Includes bibliographical references and index. | Audience: Ages: 4–8. | Audience: Grades: K to Grade 3.
Identifiers: LCCN 2016018672 (print) | LCCN 2016028641 (ebook) | ISBN 9781512425642 (lb : alk. paper) | ISBN 9781512429220 (pb : alk. paper) | ISBN 9781512427431 (eb pdf)
Subjects: LCSH: Easter—Juvenile literature.
Classification: LCC GT4935 .S36 2017 (print) | LCC GT4935 (ebook) | DDC 394.2667—dc23

LC record available at https://lccn.loc.gov/2016018672

Manufactured in the United States of America
1 — VP — 12/31/16

Expand learning beyond the printed book. Download free, complementary educational resources for this book from our website, www.lerneresource.com.

Table of Contents

Easter Sunday

Easter is a holiday.

It is always on a Sunday.

It can be in March

or April.

People all around the
world celebrate Easter.
It is a religious holiday.
Some people go
to church.

People spend time with family.

Families eat big meals.

Many people eat ham on Easter.

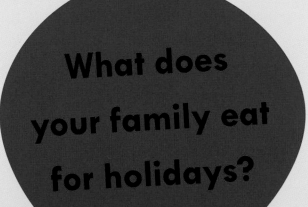

What does your family eat for holidays?

Eggs are a symbol

of Easter.

People dye Easter eggs.

We decorate eggs

with bright colors.

People decorate their homes.

They set out eggs and lilies.

Why do you think people decorate for holidays?

12

Some families hide Easter eggs.

Kids take part in Easter egg hunts.

They have fun looking for the eggs.

Bunnies are symbols of Easter too. Some people say the Easter Bunny brings gifts.

Can you think of other Easter symbols?

Easter baskets are filled with gifts.

Chocolate bunnies are popular

Easter treats.

Families celebrate Easter

in different ways.

Does your family

celebrate Easter?

Easter Symbols

Easter candy

Easter eggs

Easter basket

lilies

ham dinner

bunny

Picture Glossary

dye

to change the color of something

lilies

plants with flowers that are shaped like trumpets

religious

of or about religion, or the belief in a god

symbol

an object or picture that stands for something else

23

Index

Read More

Bullard, Lisa. *Emma's Easter*. Minneapolis: Millbrook Press, 2012.

Pettiford, Rebecca. *Easter*. Minneapolis: Bullfrog Books, 2015.

Smith, Mary-Lou. *Celebrate Easter*. New York: Cavendish Square Publishing, 2016.

Photo Credits